Common Errors in English

Paul Hancock

Penguin Quick Guides Series Editors:
Andy Hopkins and Jocelyn Potter

Pearson Education Limited
Edinburgh Gate
Harlow
Essex CM20 2JE, England
and Associated Companies throughout the world.

ISBN 0 582 46894 9

First published 2004
3 5 7 9 10 8 6 4 2

Copyright © Paul Harrock 2004

The moral right of the author has been asserted.

Produced for the publisher by Bluestone Press, Charlbury, UK.
Designed and typeset by White Horse Graphics, Charlbury, UK.
Illustrations by Anthony Maher (Graham-Cameron Illustration).
Photography by Patrick Ellis.
Printed and bound in China NPCC/03

Published by Pearson Education Limited in association with
Penguin Books Ltd, both companies being subsidiaries of Pearson plc.

For a complete list of the titles available from Penguin English visit
our website at www.penguinenglish.com, or please write to your local
Pearson Education office or to: Penguin English Marketing Department,
Pearson Education, Edinburgh Gate, Harlow, Essex CM20 2JE.

Contents

Getting started

How can this book help you?

Everyone who learns English makes the same mistakes at first, and this book shows you examples of these mistakes and how to correct them. Many of the mistakes are illustrated, so you can see exactly what people are really saying when they make them! This helps you to understand why they're wrong, and to stop making them.

What's in this book?

There are ten chapters covering different areas, such as travel, work, education and family. Each chapter has five sections and altogether there are more than 300 examples of typical mistakes, including confused words, prepositions and grammar. There are also **Review** exercises to give

you more practice in noticing mistakes and
saying what you want to say correctly.

Why is it called a *Quick Guide*?

The explanations of the mistakes are short and
simple. Each page can be studied on its own, and
because there are not too many examples on one
page, you can choose any page and spend a few
minutes learning about those mistakes. You'll
learn more by doing some quick study like this
regularly. Try looking at a few mistakes every day
and see how you begin to remember them.

How to use the book

- Choose a section which interests you. Enjoy
  the illustration and then read the explanation
  and the other examples on that page.

The following symbols are used:

✗ a sentence containing an error

! a sentence that is not incorrect but is often used incorrectly

✔ a correct sentence.

- Look at the mistakes again and cover the explanations so that you can't see them. Can you remember why it's a mistake and how to correct it? Keep testing yourself like this until you remember and are ready to move on to another section.

- Do the **Review** exercises and check the **Answers** section at the back of the book.

- Go to the **Index** and write down the examples in your own language.

I hope you find the book both useful and amusing!

Moving
around

1

Away from home

✗ It was interesting to have class discussions with other **strangers**.

stranger

foreigner

Strangers are people you've never met before. People of other nationalities are **foreigners**, but this is often used negatively, so avoid it. *We don't want foreigners here!*

usual

common

✔ It was interesting to have class discussions with **people from other countries**.

strange

foreign

✗ John is a very **usual** name in Britain.

For *many* examples of something, say **common**, not **usual**.

✔ John is a very **common** name in Britain.

There were a lot of strange students in the class.

✗ There were a lot of **strange** students in my class.

Something **strange** is not normal and makes you uncomfortable. Students from other countries are **foreign** students.

✔ There were a lot of **foreign** students in my class.

Travel

! I love travel.
When you are speaking generally, it is more common to say:

travel | ✔ I love travelling.

---

journey | ✘ I'm going on a business travel next week.
trip | **Travel** is uncountable (without *a*). You can *go on* or *make* **a journey**. If you go and come back after a short time, it's called **a trip**.
tour |
street | ✔ I'm going on a business trip next week.
road |

---

flight | ✘ We went on a journey round the city by bus.
If you visit a lot of different places by bus, it is called a **tour**.

✔ We went on a bus tour round the city.

✗ The streets between Oxford and Bath are beautiful.

Streets are in towns and villages, with houses on them. Between towns, there are **roads**.

✓ The roads between Oxford and Bath are beautiful.

Did you have a good voyage?

❗ Did you have a good voyage?

Voyage is an old-fashioned word for long journeys by ship.

✓ Did you have a good journey/flight?

Here and there

✘ I'll have to **bring** a lot of books with me when I **come back** to France.

This is wrong if you're in Britain and talking to someone in Britain. You usually **come** to and **bring** things to the place where you are speaking.

✔ I **brought** a lot of clothes with me when I **came** to England.

BRITAIN

✔ I'll have to **take** a lot of books with me when I **go back** to France.

come
(back)

bring

take

go
(back)

You usually **go** to and **take** things to a different place from the place where you are speaking.

If you're talking to someone about a time when you will be in another place, you can use **come** and **bring**.

✔ I'll have to **bring** a lot of books with me when I **come back** to Italy.

✔ You must **come** and visit me in Rome.

Outside world

nature

the country

landscape

scenery

camping

campsite

shadow

shade

✗ I love going for walks in **nature**.

Nature is the world of plants and animals that biologists study. If you love fields and trees, you go for walks in **the country**.

✔ I love going for walks in **the country**.

❗ The **landscape** in the Lake District is very beautiful.

Landscape is normally used by artists or geographers. When you go to the country you enjoy the beautiful **scenery**.

✔ The **scenery** in the Lake District is very beautiful.

✗ We found a **camping** near the town.

A place to put a tent is a **campsite**.

✔ We found a **campsite** near the town.

My boyfriend sat in the sun and I sat in the shadow.

✘ I sat outside in the **shadow**.

A **shadow** is made by your body or your hand and is too small to sit in. If it's too hot, you sit in the **shade** (made by something bigger – a building or a tree, for example).

✔ I sat outside in the **shade**.

Small words

✘ She goes to work **with her car**.
This means that the car accompanies you!
You go to work **by car** (without *my*, *her*, etc.).

✔ She goes to work **by car**.

by car

on foot

✘ You can get to the hotel **by foot**.
You go **by car**, **by plane**, etc., but **on foot**.

✔ You can get to the hotel **on foot**.

come to

arrive at

✘ I hope you'll **come in Spain** soon.
You can come and go **in** a room or house.
You travel **to** a country or town.

in front of

opposite

✔ I hope you'll **come to Spain** soon.

✘ She **arrived to** the office late.
You can never arrive **to** a place. You can arrive
in a town or country, or **at** other places.

✔ She **arrived** late **at** the office **in** Pisa.

There's a cinema in front of my house.

! There's a cinema **in front of** my house.

If there's a cinema on the other side of the road, say:

✔ There's a cinema **opposite** my house.

Review 1

A Choose the correct answer.

1 I really love (*travel/ travelling*).
2 I enjoy long train (*voyages/ journeys*).
3 I'm coming to Rome on a business (*trip/ travel*).
4 Could you give me a (*tour/ journey*) of the city?
5 I'm in Lyon. I hope you can (*go/ come*) here soon.
   (*Take/ Bring*) your family with you.
6 We often have (*strangers/ foreigners/ people from
   other countries*) staying with us.
7 Those clothes are very (*usual/ common*) in Japan.

B Complete these sentences.

1 Only the English sit in the sun in summer.
   The locals sit in the ..... .
2 Are you coming .... car or .... foot?
3 I went .... America last year.
4 They arrived .... the station just in time.

School
and
work

2

Education

student

child

professor

teacher

learn

teach

class

classroom

✗ When I started school aged seven, there were 20 **students** in my class.

Students are older learners, over 16 and usually at university. In school there are **schoolchildren** or just **children** (**pupils** is more formal).

✔ ... there were 20 **children** in my class.

✗ My school **professors** were friendly.

Only universities have **professors** or **lecturers**. Schools have **teachers**.

✔ My school **teachers** were friendly.

✗ My English teacher **learnt** me a lot.

Teachers **teach** you things and you **learn** them.

✔ My English teacher **taught** me a lot.

There are some nice pictures in my class.

✗ There are some nice pictures in my **class**.

The **class** is the group of people learning. The place where you learn is the **classroom**.

✔ There are some nice pictures in my **classroom**.

27

Work and jobs

I work like
a waitress
on Fridays.

✗ I **work like** a waitress on Fridays.

In **work like**, *like* means *similar to* e.g. *I work like a slave!* To tell someone your position at work, use **as**.

✔ I **work as** a waitress on Fridays.

✗ I have a good **work**.

Work is uncountable. You can finish **some work** and then do some different work. A **job** (architect, teacher etc.) is the same every day.

✔ I have a good **job**.

✗ I go **to my work** by bicycle.

You go **to work**, without *my*, *your*, *his* etc.

✔ I go **to work** by bicycle.

! What's your **occupation**, David?

Occupation is a formal word, usually used in writing (official forms etc.). Use **job**.

✔ What's your **job**?/What do you do?

work as

work

job

occupation

Companies

There are two chiefs in my office.

✗ There are two **chiefs** in my office.

You can have a *chief executive*, or *chief accountant*, but a **chief** is usually the leader of a tribe of American Indians. At work you have a **boss** or a **manager**.

✔ There are two **managers** in my office.

✗ The **labourers** have asked the **managers** for more money.

In industry, pay and conditions are discussed by **workers** and **management**.

✔ The **workers** have asked the **management** for more money.

chief

manager

worker

management

work in/for

personal

personnel

✗ I **work in** a finance company.

Use **in** to say where exactly you work in a company, e.g. *in the accounts department*. To tell someone about your employer:

✔ I **work for** a finance company.

✗ I work in the **personal** department.

Personal means connected with your private life, e.g. *Can I ask you a personal question?*

The department that helps individuals at work is the **personnel** department.

✔ I work in the **personnel** department.

31

Money

If you pay the food, I'll buy the drinks.

✗ If you **pay** the food, I'll buy the drinks.

You have to **pay** someone **for** something when you buy it.
(You can *pay the bill* and *pay tax* because you don't buy
these things.)

✔ If you **pay for** the food, I'll buy the drinks.

✗ Doctors get a good **wage**.

Some workers, usually doing physical jobs, get a *weekly* wage. Most people nowadays, especially professionals, get a *monthly* **salary**.

✔ Doctors get a good **salary**.

✗ We'll have to **rise** the price of this product.

A price **rises** when it increases, but if someone increases a price, they **raise** the price.

✔ We'll have to **raise** the price of this product.

✗ The **price of living** is very high in London.

You pay a **price** in order to have something. To say how expensive a city or country is, we say:

✔ The **cost of living** is very high in London.

pay for

wage

salary

rise

raise

price

cost of living

Words that go together

I never do mistakes in English!

✗	✔	
We don't **do** a mistake.	We **make** a mistake. We **make** a speech. We **make** a phone call.	
We don't **make** an exercise.	We **do** an exercise. We **do** a job or some work. We **do** business with somebody.	**make** **do** **take**
We don't **make** an exam.	We **take** an exam. We **take** a course. We **take** a day off work.	**have**
We don't **make** an interview.	We **have** an interview. We **have** a lesson. We **have** a meeting.	

Review 2

A Choose the correct answer.

1 My geography (*professor*/*teacher*) at school was very nice. She (*taught*/*learnt*) us a lot.

2 What (*do you do*/*are you doing*)? – I work (*in*/*for*) a television company.

3 Jane has two (*jobs*/*works*). She works (*like*/*as*) a secretary and in a café.

4 He's the (*chief*/*boss*), but he goes (*to his*/*to*) work by bicycle.

5 Teachers get a good (*salary*/*wage*) in Japan, but the (*cost*/*price*) of living is also higher there.

B Complete these with *make, take* or *have*.

1 Can you …. this exam without …. any mistakes?

2 If you …. that exam, you'll …. an interview to test your spoken English.

3 I can't …. a phone call now, we're …. a meeting.

Home
life

3

Family

✗ I **am born** in Madrid.

In English we see this only as a past action.

✔ I **was born** in Madrid.

---

born

grow (up)

parent

relative

strong

strict

✗ Your children are much taller – they really have **grown up**.

To **grow up** means to become an adult and act like one.

✔ I want to be a nurse when I **grow up**.

When children get *physically bigger*, say:

✔ Your children are much taller – they really have **grown**.

✗ I have many **parents** in my town.

You can only have two **parents**. Other family members are **relatives**.

✔ I have many **relatives** in my town.

My father was very strong with us as children.

✘ My father was very **strong** with us as children.

If someone is **strong**, it's a physical characteristic. A person who makes children follow rules is **strict**.

✔ My father was very **strict** with us as children.

Home and away

I'm resting at my friend's house all week.

✗ I'm **resting** at my friend's house all week.

You **rest** when you're tired. If you're living in someone's house, use **stay**.

✔ I'm **staying** at my friend's house all week.

✗ I'm tired. I want to go to **my house**.

You only say **my house** if you are choosing, e.g. *Shall we go to my house, or to yours?* When you are tired, you want to go **home**.

✔ I'm tired. I want to go **home**.

❗ See you later. I'll **return home** at about eight.

Return home and **arrive home** are formal. Informally you can say:

✔ I'll **be home** at about eight. (I'll **get home**/I'll **come home** …)

rest

stay

house

home

Guests for dinner

I really love the French kitchen.

✗ I really love **the French kitchen**.
The **kitchen** is the room where you cook! You can say **French cuisine**, but you usually say:

✔ I love **French food**. (without *the*)

kitchen

food

✗ My sister is a very good **cooker**.
A **cooker** is a machine (gas or electric)! A person who cooks is a **cook**.

✔ My sister is a very good **cook**.

cooker

cook

! The guests will be here soon. I'll just **clean** the living room.
We usually **clean** using water. You can quickly **tidy** a room by putting everything in its place.

✔ I'll just **tidy** the living room.

clean

tidy

Meals

Delicious! This is my favourite plate!

✘ Delicious! This is my favourite **plate**!

The thing you put food on is called a **plate**. When you cook food in a particular way, it's called a **dish**.

✔ This is my favourite **dish**!

! Pizza followed by ice-cream – that's my favourite **food.**

Food is what you buy and can use to make your favourite **meal**. A meal can have one, two, three or more **courses**.

✔ Pizza followed by ice-cream – that's my favourite **meal.**

✘ Would you like some **desert**?

A **desert** is a place that's all sand, e.g. *the Sahara desert*. The sweet thing you eat at the end of a meal is the **dessert**.

✔ Would you like some **dessert**?

✘ We don't usually **eat a breakfast.**

All meals are without **a** (*breakfast*, *lunch* and *dinner*). Also, you usually say you **have breakfast**, not **eat** it.

✔ We don't usually **have breakfast.**

plate

dish

meal

desert

dessert

have breakfast

Small words

care about

take care of

married to

good at

look for

look after

✗ When my mother went to work, my aunt **cared about** us.

To **care about** someone means to have feelings for them. If you're physically responsible for someone you **take care of** them.

✔ ... my aunt **took care of** us.

✗ I didn't know that Anna was **married with** Paul.

You can **live with** someone, but you are **married to** somebody.

✔ I didn't know that Anna was **married to** Paul.

✗ My sister is very **good in** cooking.

People are good or bad **at** something.

✔ My sister is very **good at** cooking.

Jim's away, so I'm looking for his houseplants.

✗ Jim's away, so I'm **looking for** his houseplants.

If you **look for** something, you try to find it. If you are responsible for something, you **look after** it.

✔ ... so I'm **looking after** his houseplants.

Review 3

Complete the gaps.

I (1) .... born in Lisbon. My mother had to leave
(2) .... very early to go to work and she didn't
(3) .... home until late, so my grandmother
looked (4) .... us children during the day.
Sometimes we (5) .... at my grandmother's house
for the night, but when I was small, I cried
because I wanted to go (6) ..... . Later, I enjoyed
going to her (7) .... , much more than going to
my other (8) .... houses, because although she
was quite (9) .... with us when we behaved badly,
she was good (10) .... playing with children.
When I grew (11) .... and left (12) .... to go to
university, my grandmother was very sad. She
was very happy when I got married
(13) .... a boy who lived near her house!

People

4

Character

I have good relations with my father.

✘ I have **good relations** with my father.

In politics, countries can have good relations with each other.
With family and friends you have a **good/bad relationship**.

✔ I have a **good relationship** with my father.

✗ I've never met your sister – **how is she?**

You only ask *How is she?* if you know her. The answer might be *She's fine/very well*. To ask about the character of someone you don't know, ask:

✓ … **what's she like?**

✗ I enjoyed meeting your brother at the party – he's very **sympathetic**.

A **sympathetic** person understands your problems and feels sorry for you. A person who is easy to like, is very **nice** or **likeable**.

✓ … he's very **nice**.

✗ It takes a few days to **know** new people.

First you have to **get to know** new people. After that, you **know** them.

✓ It takes a few days to **get to know** new people.

relations

relationship

what's she like?

sympathetic

nice

get to know

Describing people

My friend is two metres high!

✘ My friend is two metres **high**!
You can talk about a person's **height**, but you say someone is two metres **tall**.

✔ My friend is two metres **tall**!

✘ I'm very tall, but my mother and father are both quite **small**.
Small is the opposite of **big** or **large**. The opposite of **tall** is **short**.

✔ ... my mother and father are both quite **short**.

✘ I've got brown **hairs**.
You only say **hairs** if you can count them, e.g. *There are two hairs in my soup!* The **hair** on your head is usually uncountable.

✔ I've got brown **hair**.

✘ My daughter **has 16 years**.
You can **have** years of experience, but you say someone **is** 16 (**years old**).

✔ My daughter **is 16**.

high

tall

small

short

hairs

hair

53

Clothes

trousers

match

suit

fit

cloth

clothes

✘ **This trouser** is nice.

You can say **a pair of trousers**, or **these trousers** (plural).

✔ **These trousers** are nice.

✘ That dress really **matches** you.

Your jacket can **match** your trousers, if the colours are similar. If something you wear looks good on you, it **suits** you.

✔ That dress really **suits** you.

✘ This is the right size – it **suits** me perfectly.

If something you wear is the right size, you say it **fits** you.

✔ This is the right size – it **fits** me perfectly.

I hope I can find a nice cloth to wear.

✗ I hope I can find **a nice cloth** to wear.

A **cloth** is a piece of material. People wear **clothes**, but there is no singular. You have to say *a dress*, *a suit* etc. In formal language you can talk about an item of clothing.

✔ I hope I can find **some nice clothes** to wear.

Communication

watch

see

say

tell

explain

hear

listen to

✗ I **watched** a car accident yesterday.

To **watch** also means you decide to give your attention to something for some time. You **see** something even if you don't want to.

✔ I **saw** a car accident yesterday.

✗ He **said me** that I was wrong.

You usually use **say** without *me, you* etc.: *He said that I was wrong.* You can talk about what someone **said to you**: *He said hello to me.* If someone gives you information, you say *He told me that I was wrong* (without *to*).

✔ He **said** that I was wrong./He **told me** that I was wrong.

✗ She **explained me** the problem.

You have to say:

✔ She **explained** the problem **to me**.

I often hear jazz at home.

! I often **hear** jazz at home.

When you **hear** something, you don't decide to, it just comes to your ears. When you decide to give your attention for a longer period of time, you **listen to** something.

✔ I often **listen to** jazz at home.

Small words

Peter reminded me of the chicken in the oven.

✗ Peter **reminded me of** the chicken in the oven.

If you are **reminded of** someone or something, you think of it because there's a similarity, e.g. *Peter reminds me of my brother – they have very similar faces*. If you want to be sure someone doesn't forget something, you **remind** them **about** it.

✔ Peter **reminded me about** the chicken …

✗ I put the tent up all **by my own**.

If there is nobody to help you, you do things **on your own** or **by yourself**.

✔ I put the tent up all **on my own**.

❗ Our secretary is **thinking about** leaving.

If you're **thinking about** something, it is happening in your head at this moment, e.g. *You look worried, Steven. What are you thinking about?* If you have a plan but you're not sure about it yet, you are **thinking of** doing it.

✔ Our secretary is **thinking of** leaving.

✗ That's my friend on the other side of the street. I'll **shout at** him.

You **shout at** someone when you're angry. To attract someone's attention, you **shout to** them.

✔ ... I'll **shout to** him.

remind me of

remind me about

on my own

think about

think of

shout

Review 4

Complete each sentence with these phrases.

1 a good relationship/good relations
   a) Britain has .... with Argentina now.
   b) Barbara has .... with her boss.

2 How is she?/What's she like?
   a) I don't know Jimmy's wife. ....
   b) I'm looking forward to seeing Mary again. ....

3 sympathetic/nice
   a) Trevor listens to your problems – he's very .....
   b) Jill has many friends – she's a very .... person.

4 fits/suits
   a) You look good in that jacket. It really .... you.
   b) This shirt is the right size. It .... me perfectly.

5 hear/listen to
   a) I think I .... somebody crying!
   b) Jack's playing piano at the pub this evening
   and we're going to .... him.

Problems

5

Losing things

Someone stole a house in London yesterday.

✘ Someone **stole** a house in London yesterday.

If you **steal** something, you *take it away*. Burglars **burgle** houses, robbers **rob** banks and thieves **steal** things from people.

✔ Someone **burgled** a house yesterday.

✗ I've **forgotten** my lunch at home!

You can say *I've forgotten to bring my lunch!* but you **leave** things in another place.

✔ I've **left** my lunch at home.

✗ Annette **remembered** me to bring some cups.

You **remember to do** something, but you **remind another person** to do it.

✔ Annette **reminded** me to bring some cups.

✗ I hope I will learn a lot because I don't want to **lose my time**.

If you don't spend your time usefully, you **waste time**.

✔ ... I don't want to **waste my time**.

steal

rob

burgle

forget

leave

remember

remind

waste time

Difficult feelings

Young children are often frightening.

! Young children are often **frightening**.

If someone or something is frighten**ing**, bor**ing**, tir**ing** etc., they are *causing* the feeling. If you are getting the feeling from someone or something, you are frighten**ed**, bor**ed**, tir**ed** etc.

✔ Young children are often **frightened**.

frightening

frightened

✘ My boss is difficult to work for – she's always very **nervous**.

Nervous means *worried* and *lacking confidence* (usually before something important, like an exam). If someone *always* has a difficult character, you can say they are **bad-tempered**.

✔ My boss is difficult to work for – she's always very **bad-tempered**.

nervous

bad-tempered

✘ His singing is **making me nervous**!

If someone has a bad habit, it can **get on your nerves** or **annoy** or **irritate** you.

✔ His singing is **getting on my nerves**.

get on my nerves

Life's difficulties

The people upstairs are a problem, but we just have to support them.

! The people upstairs are a problem, but we just have to **support** them.

If you have to live with something you don't like, you **put up with** it (**tolerate** is formal). **Support** means to hold something up.

✔ ... but we just have to **put up with** them.

✘ Please don't invite Robert to the party, I really **can't suffer** him.

If you dislike someone very strongly, you **can't stand** or **can't bear** them.

✔ ... I really **can't stand** him.

✘ They have a big **difficulty** with their teenage son.

You have **difficulty** or **difficulties** with something, but you can't have **a** difficulty. Use **a problem** instead.

✔ They have a big **problem** with their teenage son.

✘ The new system has **made** many **troubles** at work.

Trouble is usually uncountable, so you can't use it with *many*. You would say that something has **caused** a lot of **trouble**.

✔ The new system has **caused** a lot of **trouble** at work.

support

put up with

can't stand

difficulty

problem

cause trouble

Medical problems

Two people were wounded in the traffic accident.

✗ Two people were **wounded** in the traffic accident.

People are **wounded** in a fight or war, by guns or knives etc. If people's bodies are damaged in an accident, they are **injured**.

✔ Two people were **injured** in the traffic accident.

! Anna has been **sick** for three days.

If someone has been **sick**, it usually means they have vomited food from their stomach. When someone is not at work because of illness they are **off sick**, but generally say:

✔ Anna has been **ill** for three days.

✗ The injured were **cured** at City Hospital.

People can be **cured** of a *disease*, if the disease disappears completely. But all people in hospital are **treated** by doctors.

✔ The injured were **treated** at City Hospital.

✗ The doctor gave me a **receipt** and I took it to the pharmacy.

You get a **receipt** when you pay in a shop. A doctor gives you a **prescription**. **Pharmacy** is a formal word. We usually say the **chemist's**.

✔ The doctor gave me a **prescription** and I took it to the chemist's.

wounded

injured

sick

ill

cure

treat

receipt

prescription

Small words

The police are searching the missing teenager.

✗ The police are **searching** the missing teenager.

To **search** someone or something means to examine every part of it to look for something, e.g. *The customs officer searched the car for drugs.* If something is missing, you **search for**, or look for it.

✔ The police are **searching for** the missing teenager.

search

search for

! We practised **throwing** the ball **at** each other.

You throw something **at** someone aggressively, e.g. *Never throw stones at people!* If you want to be helpful, you can throw something **to** somebody.

throw at

throw to

kill by

kill with

✔ She **threw** the ball **to** me.

! The man was **killed by** a knife.

The man was killed **with** a knife, **by** the person using it.

✔ The man was **killed with** a knife.

Review 5

Choose the correct word(s).

I find my work very (1) *interested/interesting* so I don't mind (2) *putting up with/supporting* the other people in the office. One of my colleagues is a very (3) *nervous/bad-tempered* person and another one really (4) *gets on my nerves/makes me nervous* with his stupid jokes. It's the boss I really can't (5) *suffer/stand*, though, because she's always (6) *making/causing* trouble. Last week her personal assistant was so (7) *ill/sick* that she ended up being (8) *treated/cured* in hospital. But the only thing the boss could talk about was what a big (9) *difficulty/problem* it is when people are off work!

Time

6

When exactly?

BISTRO · MAY · 18 ·

We're meeting in May 18th.

✗ I'll see you **in Monday** morning.

You say **in the morning**, but **on Monday**, so you say **on Monday morning**.

✔ I'll see you **on Monday** morning.

✗ We're meeting **in May 18th**.

You say **in May** but **on the 18th**, so you say **on May 18th**.

✔ We're meeting **on May 18th**.

✗ Your grandmother is coming **on next Thursday**.

You don't use a preposition before **next**.

✔ Your grandmother is coming **next Thursday**.

! The conference is **next** Thursday – **the day after tomorrow**.

If you're talking about **this** week, you say *this Thursday*. **Next** Thursday is the following week.

on
Monday

in May

on May
18th

next
Thursday

the day
after
tomorrow

75

Planning time

I've written my doctor's appointment in my agenda.

AGENDA

'Skopso' Production Team
Agenda for Meeting 18/2/01

1 January's production figures
2 Targets for March
3 New product plans

   Doctor's appointment
   Tuesday 3.15

4 Any other business

✗ I've put my doctor's appointment in my **agenda**.

An **agenda** is a list of things to be discussed at a meeting.
You write your appointments in a **diary**.

✔ I've put the appointment in my **diary**.

✗ Top managers have busy **timetables**.

Timetables are for buses or trains and schools. People have busy **schedules**.

✔ Top managers have busy **schedules**.

✗ We've received the **schedule** for your tour of Germany.

The plan for travelling to many places on a tour is called an **itinerary**.

✔ We've received the **itinerary** for your tour of Germany.

! I'm afraid the manager is **occupied** at the moment.

We say a place (e.g. an office) is occupied when people are in it. **Occupied** is rather formal for people. We say they are **busy** or **unavailable**.

✔ I'm afraid the manager is **busy** at the moment.

agenda

diary

timetable

schedule

itinerary

occupied

busy

Periods of time

I usually go skiing for the winter.

! I go skiing **for** the winter.

For tells you how long something happens, **during/in** tells you when it happened.

✔ I go skiing for two weeks **during/in** the winter.

✗ She's lived here **since** three years.

Use **since** to say when a present action began, e.g. *since 1997, since Monday*. To talk about periods of time *(how long)*, use **for**, e.g. *for three years, for four days*.

✔ She's lived here **for** three years.

✗ They went to live in the States **before two years**.

To say how long something happened *before now*, use **ago**.

✔ They went to live in the States **two years ago**.

for

during

since

ago

! David's been here **since** six months **ago**.

We don't usually use **since** with **ago**. You can say either of these.

✔ David came here six months **ago**.

✔ David's been here **since** July.

Night time

We often go for a meal in the night.

! We often go for a meal **in the night**.

If something happens **in the night**, it's when you are
sleeping (or it wakes you up). You can go for a meal **in the
evening** (between about 6 pm and 10 pm).

✔ We often go for a meal **in the evening**.

! What time do you go to bed **in the evening**?

You usually do things **in the evening**, and go to bed **at night**.

✔ What time do you go to bed **at night**?

✗ Did you go out **yesterday night**?

We never say *yesterday night* or *last evening*. We say **yesterday evening**, which is earlier than **last night**.

✔ Did you go out **yesterday evening/ last night**?

✗ **Goodnight**, Mr Stevens. Can I introduce you to my wife?

Goodnight means **goodbye** when you leave someone at night. When you meet someone formally in the evening, you say **Good evening**.

✔ **Good evening**, Mr Stevens. Can I introduce you to my wife?

night

evening

yesterday evening

last night

goodnight

good evening

New and old

Of course, everyone wants to buy the last mobile phone.

✘ Of course, everyone wants to buy **the last** mobile phone.

The mobile phone with the newest developments is the **latest** mobile phone.

✔ Everyone wants **the latest** mobile phone.

✗ We bought this computer system last year and it's already **old-fashioned**.

Old-fashioned means belonging to an older period. Something can be quite new, but if it's not the latest technology, it's **out of date**.

✔ Our computer system is **out of date**.

! Mr Zapdos is the **actual** President.

Actual means **real** (not imagined or planned) e.g. *They said the bridge would cost £4m, but the actual cost was £6m*. The President now is the **current** or **present** President.

✔ Mr Zapdos is the **current** President.

✗ They lived in Rome for a few years, but **actually** they're in Pisa.

Actually means **in fact** and is used to correct a wrong idea, e.g. *She's not my wife – she's my girlfriend, actually*. To say what someone is doing **now** …

✔ … they're in Pisa **at the moment**.

last

latest

old-fashioned

out of date

actual

current

actually

at the moment

Review 6

Complete each sentence with these words.

1 in/on
   a) I'll see you .... the morning.
   b) She's leaving .... Monday morning.

2 agenda/diary
   a) I'll check her birthday – it's in my .... .
   b) This is important. Put it on the .... for the next meeting.

3 during/for
   a) I was in England .... three weeks.
   b) He learnt to swim .... the summer.

4 for/since
   a) I've been working here .... three years.
   b) He's lived in France .... 1998.

5 Goodnight/Good evening
   a) .... and welcome to the Royal Albert Hall.
   b) .... ! Sleep well!

Linkers

7

Begin and end

At last I will end my talk …

✘ **At first** we had soup.

At first tells you how something begins, but it changes and doesn't finish this way.

✔ **At first** it was easy, but then it became difficult.

For an action that happens and finishes before another one, say:

✔ **First** we had soup.

✗ We spent two hours trying to find the restaurant. **At the end** we went home.

At first

first

> You can only say **at the end** (or **beginning**) of something, e.g. a book/film, or a holiday.
> If a situation changes and ends in an unexpected way, you can use **in the end**.

at the end

✔ We spent two hours trying to find the restaurant. **In the end**, we went home.

in the end

at last

! **At last**, I will end my talk with some statistics.

finally

> **At last** means that you have waited too long for something.

✔ We waited over 25 minutes at the bus stop. **At last**, a bus came.

> For the last of a number of actions, use **finally**.

✔ **Finally**, I will end my talk with some statistics.

One after another

after
...ing

after that

afterwards

✗ **After switching** the light on, **the computer** stopped working.

You can only use **After ...ing** if the *same subject* does both actions in the sentence.

✔ **After switching** the light on, **I** closed the curtains.

You have to use both subjects if they are different, and past tenses as usual.

✔ **After I** switched the light on, **the computer** stopped working.

✗ We saw a really good film. **After,** we went for a pizza.

After talking about one action, introduce another with **After that**, or **Afterwards**.

✔ We saw a really good film. **Afterwards,** we went for a pizza.

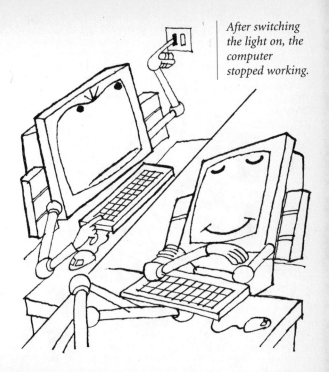

After switching the light on, the computer stopped working.

There were so many problems with booking our holiday.

✗ Goodbye. I'll come back again **after three weeks**.

To say how long before something will happen in the future, use **in … (time)**.

✔ Goodbye, I'll come back again **in three weeks' time**.

✗ There were so many problems with booking the holiday. **After all**, we decided to cancel it.

After all means you shouldn't forget this important point:

✔ I don't think Daniel should be allowed out late – **after all**, he's only 16.

If things happen to make you change plans, say:

✔ **In the end** we decided to cancel it.

in … time

after all

in the end

Saying more

Sally's coming. Furthermore, she's bringing Jane.

! Sarah speaks German well. She speaks French **also**.

Also usually comes before the verb (but after *to be*).

✔ Sarah speaks German well. She **also** speaks French.

At the *end* of a sentence, you can use **too** or **as well**.

✘ Great! Sally's coming to the party. **Furthermore**, she's bringing Jane!

Furthermore is used in more formal language to introduce another idea.

✔ The proposed bridge would be more efficient. **Furthermore**, it would have cost advantages.

When you're speaking informally, it's better to use **What's more …**

✔ Great! Sally's coming to the party. **What's more**, she's bringing Jane!

also

furthermore

what's more

Opposite ideas

Your mother's starting to look old. On the other side, she's still beautiful.

✗ Your mother's starting to look old. **On the other side**, she's still beautiful.

An argument does have two sides, but we say:

✔ … **On the other hand**, she's still beautiful.

✘ The film was too long. **Although** I did enjoy it.

Although links opposite ideas *in one sentence*.

✔ **Although** the film was too long, I did enjoy it.

✘ It's a nice car, **however** it's expensive.

Use **but** in informal language: *It's a nice car, but it's expensive.* **However** (more formal) goes with the second opposite idea in another sentence.

✔ We understand your problem. **However**, we can't help.

✘ **Despite of** the problem, we managed to finish on time.

Don't use **of** after **despite**.

✔ **Despite** the problem, we …

Or you can say:

✔ **In spite of** the problem, we …

on the other hand

although

however

despite

in spite of

95

Why?

✗ My mother spilt ketchup on my dress **so that** I had to wear a different one.

So that means to do one thing because you want another thing to happen. Use **so** (with a comma (,) before it) for a result that perhaps no-one wanted.

✓ My mother spilt ketchup on my dress, **so** I had to wear a different one.

so that

so

to do

for doing

✗ I came here **for learning** English.

If you want to say *why* you do something, use **to do**, not **for doing**.

✓ I came here **to learn** English.

✗ This knife is **to cut** meat.

You can use **for doing** to explain what something is used for.

✓ This knife is **for cutting** meat.

My mother spilt ketchup on my dress so that I had to wear a different one.

Review 7

A Correct the words in italics, if necessary.

1 *At first* we went to a pub and *afterwards* we went to a disco.
2 We spent an hour waiting for a bus. *At the end* we decided to walk.
3 Those are all the practical problems, and *at last* there is the question of cost.
4 I'm going to France *in three weeks' time*.
5 You shouldn't expect her English to be good – *after all*, she's only been learning it for a year.

B Choose the correct answer.

1 My PC crashed, (*so*/ *so that*) I called the helpline.
2 I went to town (*for doing*/ *to do*) my shopping.
3 This is called a hole-punch, because it's (*to punch holes*/ *for punching holes*).
4 Yes, it was cheap, but that wasn't the reason (*of*/ *for*) buying it.

Grammar

I

8

In the middle?

Present simple and continuous
Past simple and continuous   Stative verbs

✘ **I work** in Scotland this week.

This temporary activity will finish after a period of time, so use present continuous.

✔ **I'm working** in Scotland this week.

✘ **I'm understanding** this grammar now.

To **understand** something is permanent. Use present simple.

✔ **I understand** this grammar now.

Use past continuous when you need to say that something happened in the middle of the action.

✔ **I was living** in Italy **when I met** my wife.

For two past actions after each other, use two past simples.

✔ **I lived** in Italy for two years. **Then I came** here.

I'm selling computers.

! What **are you doing**? – **I'm selling** computers.

The present continuous here describes what is happening at the moment. For permanent routines, e.g. someone's job, use present simple.

✔ What **do you do**? – **I sell** computers.

Past and present

✗ I've been in London yesterday.

To talk about a particular time in the past, use past simple.

✔ I was in London yesterday.

! How long **are you** in Cambridge? – Since May.

If you say *How long are you in Cambridge?* you are talking about time that includes the future, e.g. *Until May.* For time including the past and present, use present perfect.

✔ How long **have you been** in Cambridge? – Since May.

✗ I've lived here **since** three years.

You say **for** a period of time and **since** a point in time.

✔ ... **for** three years; ... **since** 1998.

I've been painting three rooms today.

✗ I've been painting three rooms today.

To say how much you have done, use present perfect simple.

✔ I've painted three rooms today.

To describe activity over a period of time, use continuous.

✔ I've been painting all afternoon.

Changing habits

I'm used to driving on the left.

! I came to England in 1986. I **used to drive** on the left.

If you **used to do** something, it's a past habit that you don't do any more.

✔ I **used to drive** a French car, but I sold it.

If something was once a difficult change, but feels normal now, use *to be used to + ing.*

✔ I came to England in 1986. **I'm used to driving** on the left.

! In Brazil people **are used to drinking** a lot of coffee.

Again, use present simple to talk about people's usual way of life.

✔ In Brazil people **drink** a lot of coffee.

Use *to be used to doing* only when there is a change that makes life difficult.

✔ I can't drink coffee here in England because **I'm used to drinking** Brazilian coffee.

Futures

I'll visit our Lisbon office next week!

! **I'll visit** our Lisbon office next week!

If you use **will** to talk about future plans, it means you are deciding the plan at the moment you are speaking.

✔ The phone's ringing. **I'll get** it.

For plans you have already made, there are two possibilities:

✔ **I'm going to visit** our Lisbon office next week.

This means you've decided the plan (in your head) but *may* not have arranged it with the people in Lisbon yet.

✔ **I'm visiting** our Lisbon office next week.

This means you've definitely arranged the visit with the people in Lisbon.

✗ **When he will arrive** tomorrow, I'll speak to him.

Use a present tense after **when** to talk about the future. Use **will** for the other future action.

✔ **When he arrives** tomorrow, I'll speak to him.

If ...

Conditionals

! **When** I win the lottery, I'll buy that car.

Unless you're extremely optimistic, you probably mean:

✔ **If** I win the lottery, I'll buy that car.

It's not very likely, so you should say:

✔ If I **won** the lottery, I'd (would) buy that car.

✗ If I **will see** him, **I'll give** him your message.

You mustn't use **will** after **if**. Use a present tense and then use **will** in the other part of the sentence.

✔ If I **see** him, **I'll give** him your message.

✗ If you **would come**, you **would meet** him.

Don't use **would** after **if**. Use a past tense and **would** in the other part of the sentence.

✔ If you **came**, you **would meet** him.

✘ If you **phoned** me last week, I **would told** you.

When imagining a different past, you need more than the past simple. Use past perfect, and **would have (done)** in the other part of the sentence.

✔ If you **had phoned** me last week, I **would have told** you.

MARRIED!

If you had phoned me last week, I would have told you!

Review 8

Are these verbs correct? If not, correct them.

1 *I live* in London for a couple of months.
2 What do you do? *I'm working* in a bank.
3 *We've seen* all the tourist sights yesterday.
4 *She's interviewed* 11 people so far this morning.
5 I've just spoken to Jim. *He's coming* to dinner on Saturday night.
6 I've just checked the schedule. *I'll meet* the company president at 10 o'clock on Tuesday.
7 We'll meet you at the airport when *you will arrive*.
8 If *they would offer* me the job, I would definitely accept it.
9 If I had known, I *would have told* you.

Grammar
II

9

You mustn't get this wrong!

**Don't have to/mustn't   Must/have to
Mustn't be/can't be**

You mustn't take photos in the gallery.

✗ You **don't have to** take photos in the gallery.

If you **don't have to** do something, you can choose whether you want to do it or not.

✔ You **don't have to** come if you don't want to.

If you can't choose, say:

✔ You **mustn't/can't** take photos in the gallery.

✗ I **must to go** home soon.

Don't use **to** after **must** (or other modal verbs, e.g. *can't, should, might*).

✔ I **must go** home soon.

✗ I **must go** to the doctor's yesterday.

The past of **must** is **had to**.

✔ I **had to go** to the doctor's yesterday.

✗ That **mustn't be** Richard – he's in America.

Mustn't means that something is forbidden. If something is not possible, use **can't**.

✔ That **can't be** Richard – he's in America.

Do you or would you?

! **I like** some fruit juice. – Really! How nice.

If you **like** something, it means *always, generally*.

✔ Do you like fruit juice? – **I like** apple juice.

When offering or asking for something now, use **would like**.

✔ I'd like some fruit juice, please. – **Would you like** apple or orange?

✗ I prefer to walk today.

I prefer means always, generally. For one particular decision, use **would prefer**.

✔ I'd prefer to walk today.

✗ I prefer milk **than** cream.

When you are comparing two things with **prefer**, use **to**.

✔ I prefer milk **to** cream.

✗ I'd rather prefer to work with Anne.

You can't use **rather** and **prefer** together.

✔ I'd rather work/**I'd prefer to** work with Anne.

To or -ing? 1

✘ My boss told me I must **stop to sleep** at work.
This means you stop doing another activity, *in order* to sleep.

✔ I worked for most of the night – I just **stopped** (working) **to sleep** for two hours.

✔ My boss told me I must **stop sleeping** at work.

✘ Please **remember locking** the door.
You **remember doing** something *afterwards*. *Before*, say:

✔ Please **remember to lock** the door.

✘ Have you **tried to take** some aspirin?
This means you don't know if you can do it. If something is easy, but you don't know what the result will be, use **try** + **-ing**.

✔ Have you **tried taking** an aspirin?

The doctor suggested taking exercise.

✗ The doctor **suggested taking** exercise.

If you **suggest doing** something, you are one of the people who will do it!

✔ He **suggested that I (should) take** exercise.

To or -ing? 2

Adjectives and verbs followed by *to* + verb/-*ing*

✗ I'm **interested to take** this exam.

Interested is followed by **in**, and prepositions are always followed by do**ing**.

✔ I'm **interested in taking** this exam.

✗ I'm very **happy seeing** you.

Happy is an adjective. Adjectives are usually followed by **to** do.

✔ I'm very **happy to see** you.

✗ She **wants that I go**.

Verbs followed by a person (*me, you, him* etc.) are followed next by **to** do.

✔ She **wants me to go**.

✘ I **promised helping** him.

Some verbs are usually followed by **to do**:
promise, decide, hope, agree, refuse, manage.

✔ I **promised to help** him.

✘ I **enjoy to swim** in the sea.

Some verbs are usually followed by **doing**:
enjoy, spend time, finish, keep, avoid, practise.

✔ I **enjoy swimming** in the sea.

Word order

Position of adverbs

Adverbs can be of time (*today*), frequency (*often*), quantity (*very much*) and place (*in the garden*).

They don't go before *to be*: ✗ She (often) is ill.	They go after *to be*: ✔ She is often ill.
They don't go before *have* + verb: ✗ I (never) have seen it.	They go after *have* and before the verb: ✔ I have never seen it.
They don't go between a verb and object: ✗ They play (often) tennis. ✗ We have in Ibiza (many tourists.) ✗ I like (very much) dancing.	They go before or after them both: ✔ They often play tennis. ✔ They play tennis often. ✔ We have many tourists in Ibiza. ✔ I like dancing very much.

We have many tourists in Ibiza.

121

Review 9

Choose the correct verb form.

1 don't have to/mustn't
   a) You can take this exam if you want, but you ..... .
   b) You .... tell anybody about this, it's a secret.

2 like/would like
   a) I .... an ice-cream please.
   b) I .... most foreign food, especially Indian.

3 eating/to eat
   a) I stopped .... meat when I was 21.
   b) We walked for 4 hours and then we stopped ..... .

4 going/to go
   a) I remember .... to ballet classes when I was a child.
   b) Did you remember .... to the supermarket on the way home?

5 to use/using
   a) Have you tried .... this shampoo? It's really nice.
   b) Try .... your left hand – I know it's difficult.

Grammar
III

10

Good and well

Your garden is too beautiful.

✗ Your garden is **too** beautiful.

Too + adjective means there's a problem: *This sofa's too big to go in the room.*

✔ Your garden is **very** beautiful.

✗ He works **slow**.

You say someone is **slow** – *adjectives* tell you how someone is, looks, or seems. *Adverbs* tell you how someone *does* something.

✔ He works **slowly**.

✗ Are you **enough hungry** to eat all this?

Enough goes before nouns: *enough money, enough chairs.* But it goes after adjectives: *hungry enough, big enough.*

✔ Are you **hungry enough** to eat all this?

✗ Your house is **such tidy**.

Such + adjective come *before* the noun they describe.

✔ You have **such a tidy house**.

After nouns, use **so** + adjective.

✔ Your house is **so tidy**.

Good and better

✗ Everything is **more cheap** in this shop.

To compare short adjectives, e.g. *cheap*, *big*, *small*, say **cheaper**, **bigger**, **smaller**.

✔ Everything is **cheaper** in this shop.

✗ I prefer this car – it's **comfortabler**.

With long adjectives, e.g. *comfortable*, *interesting*, use **more comfortable**, **more interesting**.

✔ I prefer this car – it's **more comfortable**.

✗ I need a **more smaller car**.

Don't use **more** and **-er** together.

✔ I need a **smaller** car.

✗ He's **very taller** than I am.

Use **very** with adjectives, e.g. *very tall*, but **much** before comparatives.

✔ He's **much taller** than I am.

Much or many?

Little/few/a few   Much/a lot of

There were very little people on the train today.

✗ There were very **little** people on the train today.
Little with *plural nouns* means *small*, e.g. *Look at those lovely little dogs*. **Little** with *uncountable* nouns means *not much*, e.g. *I've got very little free time today*. With countable nouns, the opposite of many is **few**.

✔ There were very **few** people on the train today.

✗ My new computer has been great – I've had **a few** problems with it.
A few means quite a lot. **Few** means not enough, or less than you expected.

✔ My new computer has been great – I've had **few** problems with it.

✗ He has **much** money.
Don't use **much** in positive sentences, use it in negatives and questions.

✔ He hasn't got **much** money. Do you have **much** work to do today?
A lot of can be used with negatives, questions and in positive sentences.

✔ He has **a lot of** money.

A and the

There's a programme on TV about the dogs.

130

✘ There's a programme on TV about **the dogs**.

The dogs means some particular dogs. A TV programme would be about dogs in general, *without* the.

✔ There's a programme on TV about **dogs**.

✘ **The life** can be difficult sometimes.

In English we don't use **the** for abstract ideas such as *life*, *happiness*, *love*. Use no article.

✔ **Life** can be difficult sometimes.

✘ Chris's mother went to **prison** to visit him.

If someone goes to prison, they are a criminal (a student goes **to university** or **to school**). If you visit the building but don't receive the service, you go **to the prison** (the university or the school).

✔ Chris's mother went to **the prison** to visit him.

✘ We had **a good weather** yesterday.

You can't use **a** before **weather** and other common uncountable nouns such as *advice*, *work*, *information*, *permission*, *accommodation* and *furniture*.

✔ We had **good weather** yesterday.

Too many words!

*Nobody
can't fly.*

✗ Nobody can't fly.

You can't use two negatives (**nobody** and **can't**) together – it would make a positive!

✔ Nobody can fly.

✗ My brother he likes football.

You don't need to say **he** after you've said **my brother**.

✔ My brother likes football.

✗ I'm agree.

Agree is a verb, not an adjective, so you don't need **to be** before it.

✔ I agree.

✗ This is the book **which I bought it**.

If you use **which** to give information about something, you don't need to say **it**.

✔ This is the book **which I bought**.

Review 10

A Correct the mistakes in these sentences.

1 I like your house – it's too big.
2 I can't believe that you can read so quick.
3 Do you think the room is enough warm?
4 My salary is more higher than it used to be.
5 I've got much work to do today.

B One word in each sentence is unnecessary. Underline it.

1 The money isn't the most important thing in life – but it helps!
2 I'm going to travel for a year before I go to the university.
3 He gave me an advice on buying a car.
4 My parents they never go out.
5 I think you are agree?
6 Those are the CDs which you lent me them.

Index

Your language

actual /ˈæktʃʊəl/ p83
The actual cost of the bridge was £6m. _____

actually /ˈæktʃʊəli/ p83
It looks small but actually it's quite big. _____

after all /ɑːftərɔːl/ p91
He can't drive. After all, he's only 15. _____

after …ing /ɑːftə …ɪŋ/ p88
After seeing the film, we ate. _____

after that /ɑːftə ðæt/ p88
We saw a film. After that, we ate. _____

afterwards /ɑːftəwədz/ p88
We had lunch. Afterwards we slept. _____

agenda /ədʒendə/ p76
Here's the agenda for the meeting. _____

ago /əgəʊ/ p79
I got this computer six months ago. _____

also /ɔːlsəʊ/ p93
Ian speaks French. He also speaks Thai. _____

although /ɔːlðəʊ/ p95
Although the film was long, I liked it. _____

Your language

Your language

Your language

Your language

Your language

Your language

foreign /fɒrɪn/ p13
Oxford has a lot of foreign students. _____

foreigner /fɒrɪnə/ p12
We're all foreigners somewhere. _____

forget /fəget/ p63
I've forgotten to bring my lunch. _____

frightened /fraɪtənd/ p65
I get frightened in crowded places. _____

frightening /fraɪtənɪŋ/ p65
I find high mountains very frightening. _____

furthermore /fɜːðəmɔː/ p93
It's expensive. Furthermore it's ugly. _____

get on my nerves
/get ɒn maɪ nɜːvz/ p65
Your singing is getting on my nerves. _____

get to know /get tə nəʊ/ p51
You have to get to know people here. _____

go /gəʊ/ p17
I'm going to France next week. _____

Your language

go back /gəʊ bæk/ p17
I'm going back to my home town. _____

good at /gʊd ət/ p46
Bob is very good at cooking. _____

good evening /gʊd iːvnɪŋ/ p81
Good evening. How are you? _____

goodnight /gʊd naɪt/ p81
Goodnight. Sleep well. _____

grow /grəʊ/ p38
You're so tall! How you've grown! _____

grow up /grəʊ ʌp/ p38
I grew up in Venice. _____

hair /heə/ p53
He's got blond hair. _____

hairs /heəz/ p53
There are some hairs in my soup! _____

have /hæv/ p35
We're having a meeting on Saturday. _____

have breakfast /hæv brekfəst/ p45
I have breakfast very early. _____

Your language

Your language

in the end /ɪn ði end/ p87/91
It was raining. In the end we didn't go. _____

in ... time /ɪn ... taɪm / p91
I'll come back in three weeks' time. _____

itinerary /aɪtɪnərəri/ p77
Here's the itinerary for your trip. _____

job /dʒɒb/ p29
What's your job? What do you do? _____

journey /dʒɜːni/ p14
The journey takes two hours by car. _____

kill by /kɪl baɪ/ p71
He was killed by a drunk. _____

kill with /kɪl wɪð/ p71
He was killed with a knife. _____

kitchen /kɪtʃən/ p43
We usually eat in the kitchen. _____

landscape /lændskeɪp/ p20
He likes to paint landscapes. _____

last /lɑːst/ p82
We've got one left. This is the last one. _____

Your language

Your language

Your language

old-fashioned /əʊld fæʃənd/ p83
Her clothes are so old-fashioned! _____

on May 18th /ɒn meɪ ði eɪtiːnθ/ p75
The meeting's on May 18th. _____

on Monday /ɒn mʌndeɪ/ p75
It starts on Monday. _____

on my own /ɒn maɪ əʊn/ p59
I live on my own. _____

on the other hand
/ɒn ði ʌðə hænd/ p94
I'm old. On the other hand, I'm happy. _____

on /ɒn/ p22
He goes to work on foot. _____

opposite /ɒpəsɪt/ p23
My house is opposite the park. _____

out of date /aʊt əv deɪt/ p83
This computer is useless. It's out of date. _____

parent /peərənt/ p38
My parents are both from Scotland. _____

Your language

pay for /peɪ fə/ p32
You pay for the food. _____

personal /pɜːsənəl/ p31
Can I ask you a personal question? _____

personnel /pɜːsənel/ p31
She works in the personnel department. _____

plate /pleɪt/ p44
Be careful – don't drop those plates! _____

prescription /prəskrɪpʃən/ p69
Take this prescription to the chemist's. _____

price /praɪs/ p33
The price of food is going up. _____

problem /prɒbləm/ p67
They have a problem with their son. _____

professor /prəfesə/ p26
Professor Jones taught me at university. _____

pupil /pjuːpəl/ p26
The primary class has about 30 pupils. _____

put up with /pʊt ʌp wɪð/ p67
You have to put up with problems. _____

Your language

raise /reɪz/ p33
I asked my boss to raise my salary. _____

receipt /rɪsiːt/ p69
I've paid but I haven't had a receipt. _____

relations /rɪleɪʃənz/ p50
Spain and Italy have good relations. _____

relationship /rɪleɪʃənʃɪp/ p50
I have a good relationship with Ted. _____

relative /relətɪv/ p38
I've got relatives in the US. _____

remember /rɪmembə/ p63
I remembered to set the video. _____

remind /rɪmaɪnd/ p63
Remind me to call Josie later. _____

remind me about
/rɪmaɪnd mi əbaʊt/ p58
He reminded me about collecting John. _____

remind me of /rɪmaɪnd mi əv/ p58
This reminds me of our last holiday. _____

Your language

rest /rest/ p41
I was so tired. I just rested all day. _____

rise /raɪz/ p33
Petrol prices are rising daily. _____

road /rəʊd/ p15
The road to Chamonix is closed. _____

rob /rɒb/ p62
They robbed the bank. _____

salary /sæləri/ p33
I get paid a monthly salary. _____

say /seɪ/ p56
He said that I was wrong. _____

scenery /siːnəri/ p20
The scenery in the Alps is wonderful. _____

schedule /ʃedjuːl/ p77
Top managers have busy schedules. _____

search /sɜːtʃ/ p71
The police searched the teenagers. _____

search for /sɜːtʃ fə/ p71
They searched everywhere for their cat. _____

Your language

see /siː/ p56
I saw an accident.

shade /ʃeɪd/ p21
It's too hot. Let's sit in the shade.

shadow /ʃædəʊ/ p21
She sat in the shadow of the house.

short /ʃɔːt/ p53
She's quite short – about 1.5 metres.

shout /ʃaʊt/ p59
Stop it! Don't shout at me!

sick /sɪk/ p69
I ate something bad and was sick.

since /sɪns/ p79
She's lived here since 1999.

small /smɔːl/ p53
My car's quite small.

so /səʊ/ p96
I got there late, so I missed the start.

so that /səʊ ðət/ p96
I went upstairs so that I could be alone.

Your language

Your language

Your language

treat /triːt/ p69
The doctor's treating me for back pain. _____

trip /trɪp/ p14
I'm going to Paris on a business trip. _____

trousers /traʊzəs/ p54
I think I'll wear my green trousers. _____

usual /juːʒuəl/ p12
I'll have my usual drink, please. _____

wage /weɪdʒ/ p33
I get paid weekly. My wage isn't bad. _____

waste time /weɪst taɪm/ p63
I don't want to waste my time. _____

watch /wɒtʃ/ p56
We watched the TV last night. _____

what's more /wɒts mɔː/ p93
It's cold. What's more, it's wet. _____

what's she like? /wɒts ʃiː laɪk/ p51
Your sister? What's she like? _____

work /wɜːk/ p29
I started work at the age of 14. _____

Your language

work as /wɜːk əz/ p29
I work as a waitress in the evenings. _____

work for /wɜːk fə/ p31
I work for a computer software company. _____

work in /wɜːk ɪn/ p31
I work in the transport department. _____

worker /wɜːkə/ p31
Workers work and managers manage! _____

wounded /wuːndəd/ p68
Five soldiers were shot and wounded. _____

yesterday evening
/jestədi iːvnɪŋ/ p81
Did you go out yesterday evening? _____

Answers

Review 1
A 1 travelling   2 journeys   3 trip   4 tour   5 come/Bring
  6 people from other countries   7 common
B 1 shade   2 by/on   3 to   4 at

Review 2
A 1 teacher/taught   2 do you do/for   3 jobs/as
  4 boss/to   5 salary/cost
B 1 take/making   2 take/have   3 make/having

Review 3
1 was   2 home   3 get/come   4 after   5 stayed   6 home
7 house   8 relatives'   9 strict   10 at   11 up   12 home
13 to

Review 4
1 a) good relations   b) a good relationship
2 a) What's she like?   b) How is she?
3 a) sympathetic   b) nice
4 a) suits   b) fits
5 a) hear   b) listen to

Review 5

1 interesting   2 putting up with   3 bad-tempered
4 gets on my nerves   5 stand   6 causing   7 ill   8 treated
9 problem

Review 6

1 a) in   b) on
2 a) diary   b) agenda
3 a) for   b) during
4 a) for   b) since
5 a) Good evening   b) Goodnight!

Review 7

A 1 First/afterwards   2 In the end   3 finally
     4 in three weeks' time   5 after all
B 1 so   2 to do   3 for punching holes   4 for

Review 8

1 I am living   2 I work   3 We saw   4 correct   5 correct
6 I'm meeting   7 you arrive   8 they offered   9 correct

Review 9

1 a) don't have to   b) mustn't
2 a) would like   b) like
3 a) eating   b) to eat
4 a) going   b) to go
5 a) using   b) to use

Review 10

A 1 I like your house – it's very big.

  2 I can't believe that you can read so quickly.

  3 Do you think the room is warm enough?

  4 My salary is higher than it used to be.

  5 I've got a lot of work to do today.

B 1 <u>The</u> money isn't the most important thing in life – but it helps!

  2 I'm going to travel for a year before I go to <u>the</u> university.

  3 He gave me <u>an</u> advice on buying a car.

  4 My parents <u>they</u> never go out.

  5 I think you <u>are</u> agree?

  6 Those are the CDs which you lent me <u>them</u>.

CITY OF
SUNDERLAND COLLEGE
LEARNING CENTRE